Mia Marconi has an Italian father and an Irish mother. She grew up in London and has been a foster carer for over 20 years. During that time she has welcomed more than 250 children into her home. To protect the identities of people she is writing under a pseudonym.

Also by Mia Marconi:

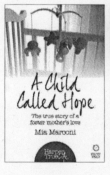

if Only He'd Told Me

if Only He'd Told Me

A foster family pushed to the limits

Mia Marconi

with Sally Beck

Certain details in this story, including names, places and dates, have been changed to protect the family's privacy.

HarperTrueLife
An imprint of HarperCollins*Publishers*
77–85 Fulham Palace Road,
Hammersmith, London W6 8JB

www.harpertrue.com
www.harpercollins.co.uk

First published by HarperTrueLife 2014

1 3 5 7 9 10 8 6 4 2

A catalogue record of this book is
available from the British Library

ISBN: 978-0-00-810510-5

Printed and bound in Great Britain by
RR Donnelley at Glasgow, UK

Chapter One

It was one o'clock in the morning when the phone jerked me out of a deep sleep. I was dreaming that I was walking down the aisle in the most gorgeous wedding dress ever made. It was cream silk overlaid with antique lace. My hair was in a chignon secured with a diamond-studded comb and my bouquet was Lily of the Valley. Martin was waiting for me at the altar with the biggest grin on his face, all four of my girls were dressed as bridesmaids and my son, looking the tidiest he had ever looked, was dressed as a page boy. I felt like a princess and was smiling so hard I was laughing. Then someone rang a bell. I thought it was the priest, but it was the phone ruining my big day.

I had no idea how long it had been ringing but I knew exactly who would be on the end of the line. There was only one organisation that phoned at the weekend and at such an unsociable hour, and that was social services.

'Good morning, Mia, it's Roz from social services. How was your sleep?'

1

I could hear the smile in her voice and had a vision of her face at the end of the line, with her great big grin and warm eyes. She immediately began giggling.

'Good morning, Roz. It's so nice to hear from you,' I said, with a slight note of sarcasm.

She went on to explain that another foster carer had been looking after a six-year-old boy who had gone berserk and smashed up her house. He'd broken everything he could, from the television to the toilet, the goldfish tank to his toys. He'd even smashed his bed and dented the fridge. Could I take him, Roz asked, because his current carer no longer wanted him in the house. He sounded more like a whirlwind than a six-year-old.

Most sane people would have said no, but this pattern of behaviour was a sign that the boy was lost and frightened, and I knew that. I also knew that this was his way of crying out for help. It wasn't very subtle, perhaps, but nevertheless I knew he needed a friend.

After an awkward silence, I said, 'How long has he been with her?' expecting a reply of two weeks.

'Two years.'

'Two years! And she wants him out of the house in the middle of a Sunday night?'

'She's hysterical, Mia, and can't stop crying. She wants him to leave now.'

'Okay,' I said. 'He can come here.'

2

'Oh, and she won't bring him herself so he's coming in a taxi with her son.'

I looked over at Martin, who was still fast asleep next to me. I had no idea how he never woke up from the noise the phone made. The dogs had started barking the second it rang and even they hadn't stirred him. World War Three could take place and I swear that man would not move.

I, on the other hand, had gone to bed knowing that I was on call for out-of-hours placements, and having fostered so many babies over the years I woke up at the drop of a nappy pin.

I got up, pulled on my dressing gown, slipped my feet into my slippers, padded downstairs, switched on the kettle and made myself a cup of tea. Jack and Jill were so over the moon to see me they nearly knocked me off my feet and began licking me, which made me laugh and calmed me down. There's nothing more therapeutic than animals, and as I sat down on the settee with my mug and pulled a blanket around me I soon felt Jack and Jill nuzzling me underneath it.

I began to think about what type of child, at only six years old, could smash up someone's home after two years. There obviously hadn't been much progress made with him if he was being this aggressive. And by the time I'd finished my tea my brain had provided me with a vision of a ten-foot-tall bruiser of a kid, complete with horns growing out of his head.

It was two o'clock in the morning by the time there was a gentle knock at the door. I opened it cautiously, expecting the worst, and could not believe my eyes. There stood a tiny olive-skinned boy, who looked about four. He was skinny but athletic at the same time, with his chest puffed out, imitating a proud rooster. His body language was cocky, bordering on the aggressive, and his full mouth was turned down and I wondered what he looked like when he smiled. His eyes were so dark they were almost black, and they were full of fear, but it took him only seconds to meet my gaze and when he did he stared right at me. No doubt this was a warning. I'm sure he was thinking, 'Don't mess with me, lady, I'm bigger than I look.'

So there was Brody, standing in front of me with two black bin bags containing his possessions. His foster carer's son was about twenty-five, a handsome young man who stood silently behind Brody looking embarrassed. His expression said: 'I can't believe it either.' He passed me the bin bags and left without saying a word.

I smiled and said to Brody: 'Are you coming in or are you going to stand there all night?' He gave me a look, pushed past me and walked into the kitchen. The dogs jumped on him. He fell to his knees and began cuddling them while they licked him from head to toe. Brody was obviously loving the attention.

4

'Sit there,' I said, pointing to the settee. I then gave him a drink of water. 'I don't know what you've done,' I began, 'but you've really upset the other carer.' He said nothing and looked defiant while I warned him. 'You're not going to start smashing up my house. There are other children here and they're asleep. I'll show you to your bedroom and I'll show you where the bathroom is and you can meet everyone tomorrow.' He nodded.

It might sound a bit harsh, and it was, but Brody had to know from the beginning that there were boundaries in our house. He would find out that I was as soft as a melting marshmallow later, but not yet.

Anyway, I was his fourth foster carer so he knew the routine, and half an hour later he was tucked up in bed fast asleep.

To an outsider, breakfast at our house would have seemed hilarious. Martin and my children came down not having a clue there was a new child in the house, but it wasn't unusual so they didn't make much of it.

'What's his name?' was all Martin whispered in my ear.

'Brody,' I whispered back before introducing him.

I already had five children of my own. Francesca, Ruby, Lucia and twins Alfie and Isabella, who were just a year younger than Brody.

Martin and Alfie were outnumbered by us girls and I smiled as I caught sight of Alfie's face. When he saw there was another boy in the house, he lit up like a firework display.

My children grabbed their breakfast and then began excitedly shooting questions at Brody as if they were a firing squad.

'How old are you?'

'Do you have brothers and sisters?'

'Are you good at football? Can you play with me after school?'

Brody obviously enjoyed the attention as his face shone like a Halloween pumpkin. Now I could see what his smile was like. He had a warm, expressive face when he was relaxed and off-guard, and he appeared confident. He looked so comfortable sitting at the kitchen table it was like he had sat in that chair all his life.

My children watched him with their eyes and mouths wide open, anticipating his answers as Rice Krispies crackled in the background. Jack and Jill sat in their usual place under the table, waiting to pounce on any scraps that fell to the floor. Their food was far too boring; they just wanted whatever the children ate and had become professional doggy hoovers. I stood by the over-worked kettle, sipping my tea, wondering why Brody had smashed his home up.

I knew I would find out later when the social

worker arrived to fill me in, but for now I couldn't see it.

My thoughts were suddenly interrupted when Alfie knocked his cereal bowl with his elbow and it hit the floor. The dogs instantly fell over each other trying to reach the contents.

'Ooops. Sorry, Mum,' Alfie said.

I rolled my eyes. 'Come on, kids. Let's get this show on the road – we have thirty minutes to get ready for school. Show Brody where all the things are to wash his face and brush his teeth.' Then I added quickly, 'Don't worry, I'll get his toothbrush.'

I knew they would all start bickering over who was going to get Brody a new toothbrush from the stack I kept for occasions just like these, and I didn't have time to referee any arguments. They all looked disappointed but I had been in this position before and I wasn't about to waste ten minutes negotiating whose turn it was to give the toothbrush to him.

Brody followed, giggling as he left the table. I smiled to myself. He seemed truly settled in.

By the time my kids had left for school, Brody had picked up one of Alfie's Transformers and was playing happily in the kitchen. There was no school for him today. We needed to meet with his social worker and get to the bottom of what was going on.

* * *

You have choices as a foster carer: the ages of children that will fit in with your family and the gender of child; whether you want to take siblings or single kids. I chose school-age children because all mine were still at school. Taking out-of-hours calls is also a choice. It could be disruptive, but I thought it was important to be there to help in emergencies.

Most carers only do this for a few months at a time, as the stress burns you out quickly. Plus, the belief you have when you first start that you're going to change the world gets lost pretty quickly. Dealing with people at their most basic and chaotic levels, who are at rock bottom and will never have that one in a million miracle transformation, and will never turn their lives around, saps your energy. It's like trying to hold back a river of treacle; eventually, the black sticky gunge will seep through the gaps.

Brody's social worker, Lottie, called just after the kids had left for school.

'I am so sorry. I can't make it until Wednesday morning,' she said.

She gave me some basic details – which school Brody went to and who his doctor was, that kind of thing – and then she asked how he was.

'It's like he's always been here,' I said, expecting her to say, 'That's fantastic!'

Instead, there was silence on the other end of the phone. She was obviously not convinced. That, or she knew something I didn't.

'I'll see you Wednesday morning,' she said and hung up.

So I was left none the wiser about the details of Brody's life, and I wondered what had led him here and whether I would be able to help him. If I was his fourth foster carer, I shouldn't kid myself that this would be an easy ride, yet I couldn't reconcile the boy who had sat happily at my kitchen table this morning with the boy capable of smashing someone's house to pieces. For the moment, I had to take him at face value and treat him the same as any other child, but nevertheless I knew not to let my guard down.

Lottie was a plump, middle-aged Jamaican lady who had a fantastic zest for life. The minute she came into my home I felt I had known her forever.

Brody was pleased to see her, which is not always the case with children and their social workers, and some will have an extremely negative response to them – one which has been drummed into them by their parents. Social workers are the baddies, they are told, the ones who take them away from their homes. If a child has this attitude it makes settling them very hard, because anything to do with social workers, including foster carers, will be tainted. It takes time to turn this attitude around, and in some cases I never manage to.

I put the kettle on – a good cup of tea is always a universal crowd pleaser. I like to use china cups and make the tea in the pot for visitors. My teapot is made of delicate bone china decorated with pink roses. It belonged to my Auntie Lily and I smile whenever I use it as it reminds me so much of her.

Brody was eager to help and keen to impress me with his willingness.

'Shall I get the sugar bowl?' he asked.

'Thank you, Brody. Can you pour some milk into Lottie's cup?'

He happily obliged while I poured the tea.

Lottie and I exchanged looks. Mine said, 'I told you he had settled well.' Hers said, 'It looks that way, but the jury is still out.'

She sat back in her chair and fumbled for papers in her rucksack.

For the next few hours we talked about Brody and she filled me in on his life. I discovered that he had been in care for a short period of time when he was a baby. This was due to reports from the hospital that he had been admitted three times for bronchitis, and because he was underweight. After meeting his parents, they put him in the category of 'failing to thrive', and he was added to the 'at risk' register.

While we were talking, sometimes Brody sat with us and at other times he ran out into the garden to kick a ball around. Each time he went outside, it gave us a chance to talk frankly about his behaviour and his background.

Lottie showed me a photo of his bedroom at home, which was so filthy it would make most people retch. Brody shared a two-bedroom flat with his parents and six siblings. His room was tiny – not so much a box room as a matchbox room – and he shared it with two of his six siblings. The other four children shared the second bedroom, while his parents slept on a sofa bed.

In his tiny, filthy, airless room there was a small window with no blinds or curtains and a frame that was black with grubby finger marks. A metal bunk bed stretched from one end of the room to the other and a camp bed was folded up and propped against the wall. How there was room to open it out I will never know. The mattresses on the bunk beds were bare, and although there were covers on the duvets it looked as though they had not been washed for a while. The saddest thing, apart from the pink carpet that was covered in unidentified black stains, was a discarded Winnie-the-Pooh toy and a sad-looking rag doll, crushed under the rungs of the camp bed.

Brody's parents were both alcohol abusers, I learned, and his mother had special needs. She was from Ghana, and any character she'd once had had been knocked out of her by Brody's father, who subjected her to domestic abuse. Not surprisingly, she had tried to kill herself several times with over-doses, and the kids had been in and out of care while she recovered in hospital, as the dad was unable to cope. His father was British, small (like Brody) and had a big mouth – one of those little men who need to be heard by everyone to give them status. Brody was his only child; the other kids who lived in the flat all had the same mother but belonged to three different men.

Along with the alcohol abuse and domestic violence, there had been allegations from the three older girls that Brody's uncle had been abusing them.

Brody was the youngest child and had been born into this chaos. It was no wonder he was bouncing off the walls.

The family were well known to social services and had been for some considerable time. There had been twenty-seven reports of concerns raised by teachers, neighbours and police. People were look-ing out for Brody and I was told that one of the teachers at his school made sure that he had a shower when he arrived at school in the mornings.

Social services had tried all the usual interven-tions with the family and all of them had failed. Brody was finally removed just before his third birthday, but by then a lot of damage had already been done. I knew that to have a real chance of a normal life Brody should have been removed as a baby. His brothers and sisters had been removed at the same time, so the whole family had been separated, which saddened me beyond belief.

The reality for large families is that not many people have the room to take groups of siblings. Whatever their parents have done and however horrific their home lives seem, to the children it is normal and they want to stick together. Their brothers and sisters are usually the only family they have left to cling to, and leaving them, as well as their parents, is a double trauma.

It was fate that brought Brody to us, although I had no idea of that when I took the emergency call. I was stunned to discover that I had been on the brink of being involved with his family on a couple of other occasions. The first was when I was pregnant with Alfie and Isabella. I got a call from social services asking me if I could look after a two-day-old girl called Destiny, but as I was about to give birth I couldn't take her. Her name was so unusual that I'd always remembered it. I didn't know then that Destiny had an older sister called Fifi. Fifi became pregnant aged fifteen, and social services called to ask if I could take a mother-and-baby placement. I couldn't at the time and it wasn't until Brody came to stay that I discovered that Fifi and Destiny were related and that they were Brody's half-sisters.

Lottie wouldn't have the full facts about what had happened with the previous carer until she'd had a chance to visit, but she warned me, looking subdued, that I was enjoying the honeymoon period with Brody.

'His behaviour can be extreme,' she said. 'He's already broken a teacher's arm and smashed up his classroom, and he has caused serious damage in all his foster carers' homes.'

I poured more tea and looked out of the window at this tiny little kid jumping up and down on the trampoline. I felt uneasy and wondered momentarily if I should refuse to keep Brody.

'Just look at him,' I said to Lottie. 'Butter wouldn't melt in his mouth. Who would have thought someone that small could cause such havoc?'

'Lottie!' Brody shouted. 'Watch me! Watch me!'

Lottie stopped and looked just as Brody executed the perfect back flip. He stood up, waited for the applause and wasn't disappointed.

Lottie sipped her tea. 'You're an experienced carer, so I'm sure you will be fine,' she said. And I thought she was probably right, so in that split second I decided to welcome Brody into our home.

Chapter Two

Just over four months had passed and Lottie had become part of our family. The children absolutely adored her and her visits were like a ray of sunshine. Screams of excitement would always fill the room when Lottie arrived, and we talked often of Brody's family. I was beginning to fill in the gaps.

Those first few months were relatively smooth, and to outsiders it was like he had always been there. His family visited once a month and Brody was always pleased to see them, but you could tell that he was disappointed too. He had his own fantasy of what family should be like, and he could see that his fell short.

When I finally met his parents I tried hard, but I never built up a relationship with either of them. To be honest, I was struggling to be civil to Brody's dad, knowing what he was like. I found making polite conversation with them difficult and they never seemed that interested to hear about Brody's achievements. No wonder he always craved attention, I thought. Their visits seemed like box ticking to me, something they had to do if they were to have a chance of getting him back, but there was no real concern for his welfare. The truth is that they didn't seem to think much of me either. To Brody's mum and dad, I was always going to be the enemy – the reason their son was no longer living with them.

School was always an issue for Brody and he found it hard to fit in, but I believed I would be able to work closely with all his teachers to make it a positive experience rather than a negative one for him. Success at school is partly about teachers' and pupils' expectations, and Brody seemed to be stuck in a vicious cycle of being labelled the worst-behaved boy in the class.

We all know from experience that school does not suit every child, and the way the system currently stands it will fail some children from the very start. It was failing Brody, and to turn that around was going to be a massive task. We needed him to be seen as a positive role model in class, and I could see this was going to take a lot of work, with nurturing at home as well as at school.

Although Brody found school a problem, at home he had found a soulmate in Alfie. They became so close they were almost like brothers. Alfie was so used to being surrounded by girls it was a breath of fresh air for him to have someone to play football with, build dens at the bottom of the garden with and ride his bike with in the local wood. It all seemed pretty perfect, a match made in heaven, a proper bromance.

A carer's children are key to helping a foster child settle in, which not everyone realises. Quite often when new children arrive the older ones are withdrawn and sullen, while the younger ones can be screaming, spitting, kicking, throwing themselves on the floor and making themselves sick. It's all fear about what will happen next, but you can see them calm down really quickly once they realise that there are other children in the house.

It's not nice for my kids to see another child hit and kick their mother, so when there's an 'incident' I make sure they're out of the way and always explain why children are acting in this way. It is still frightening, as life is sometimes, but I know my son and daughters are prepared.

I have no doubt that the fact there was a boy of a similar age to Brody in the house gave him confidence and helped him feel at home. I had seen it a hundred times before and thought back to the time when we had a two-year-old girl here called Bethany, who was very uncomfortable around bath time. Most toddlers reach up to you to be lifted in and out of the bath, but she would freeze if I tried to touch her. My girls instinctively sensed that they could help and, without me saying a word, one of them would lift her out of the bath, wrap her in a towel and give her a big cuddle. She felt comfortable with them doing it rather than me. Bethany had been badly abused by her mother, so why should she trust another female adult? But why should she miss out on one of the best things about being a child – being cuddled in a towel after a nice warm bath – because of this trauma? For weeks Francesca or Ruby would gently lift Bethany out of the bath until one day, without thinking, Bethany lifted her arms towards me. At that moment I knew we were making progress. I smiled at Francesca and Ruby to let them know that this breakthrough was thanks to them and that it might never have happened if it wasn't for their caring.

Some social workers show little interest in the children who help in foster caring, which saddens me. Thankfully, they are outnumbered by those who go out of their way to make these children feel important, so that they realise how important their contribution is.

I experience it every day, and it's lovely to watch Francesca and Ruby help our foster children with their homework. The kids always want the girls to help them, never me.

They help with more than just homework, though. I remember overhearing the girls talking to one foster child about problems at school. Martine was six at the time and she told Ruby: 'My friend's been horrible today. She said that I haven't got a real mummy.'

Quick as a flash, Ruby told her: 'Just tell her that you're luckier than everyone else because you've got two mummies and they've only got one.' Within minutes, Martine was smiling again. It's that kind of great advice that really helps these children, and it is so much more convincing coming from another child.

Watching my children follow their daily routine helps foster children learn about a normal home life. They see me reading them a bedtime story and tucking them in and kissing them goodnight and it gives them confidence that the same routine is right for them. They might not want me to be too involved, but they will happily allow my girls. Lots of foster children find that bedtime is a problem. Some find it frightening, but after Francesca or Ruby have read them a bedtime story they find it much easier to settle.

Then there's dance, which is always an ice-breaker and a bonding tool in my house. My girls love dancing to pop music and make sure they pass on their ballet and street dance skills to any child who is interested. I've lost count of how many dance shows we've had in our house.

Clothes for foster children are always a big factor too. A lot of them have never had a choice about what to wear, or any clean clothes for that matter. I've seen countless photos of children's bedrooms strewn with piles of dirty clothes. Consequently, as long as it's clean, they just pull on whatever they can find, whether that's a summer T-shirt and a pair of shorts in the middle of winter or a jumper and jeans in summer. Francesca and Ruby have always made sure they know what the right clothes to wear are and have helped them develop a sense of pride in looking clean and tidy.

The children who went to the same school as my kids saw them as positive role models there too, and they picked up their good eating habits at home, sitting down for a proper meal instead of having a bag of crisps or a bag of sweets. They watched my kids play sports, learned what it was like if someone was kind to you and how to be kind in return. I could teach them some of these skills, but watching other children was always a much more powerful lesson.

All sorts of combinations of children have lived with me: babies and toddlers, only children, single siblings and sibling groups. A major lesson I have to teach groups of siblings when they come to live with us is that the older one doesn't have to take on a parenting role for the younger ones any more. It's really hard for them to let go, because they have grown up believing they need to protect the younger children. I remember Louisa, a six-year-old girl, and her four-year-old brother Billy. Louisa did everything for Billy, including making his food. When I explained that she didn't have to look after her baby brother in that way any more, that I would do it, it was hard for her to take. Every time we went to the supermarket, if I took my eyes off Louisa for a minute she would steal a pram or a buggy. She thought all babies in prams were vulnerable and needed to be looked after in the way she'd looked after her brother. I lost count of the number of times I had to explain to a distracted parent that I was sorry, that Louisa had just made a mistake.

One solution would have been to let her push Billy in the shopping trolley, but if I had done that she would never have learned how to be a child. It was awkward, though, and she kept trying to steal babies for about two years, the last time being when we were in Italy on holiday. We were all walking single file down a narrow street, with me leading, and when I looked back Louisa was pushing a pram.

'Louisa, where did you get that from?' I cried. She looked guiltily at me and before she could answer I saw a mother outside a bar, completely hysterical.

I had told her hundreds of times not to take prams, but this time I really had to shout at her – something I hate doing, but drastic action was needed. It worked, and thankfully that was the last time she did it.

* * *

So many children who come into care have big voids in their lives. If you think of growing up in a functioning family in terms of drawing a map of childhood where you need to get from A to Z to fully develop, it might help explain what happens to these children and why so many become feral. You can't get to Z unless you follow the right path, and if you don't follow that path you end up in dark, scary woods.

As a parent, if you don't respond to babies when they smile or cry – the two simplest social interactions that are a baby's main form of communication – they don't know how to respond when someone smiles at them or is in distress. They will struggle to communicate for the rest of their lives unless they learn how, and in Brody's case smashing up the place was his way of attracting attention and saying, 'I really need you to listen.'

Brody was a feral child because his parents really didn't care. No one went to him when he cried as a baby or whined as a toddler, so his behaviour became extreme to help him get the attention he needed.

He was manipulative too. To everyone on the perimeter of our family Brody was a charmer, a friendly lad who was the first to offer help at parties. There was Brody, folding up the tables and chairs, taking the rubbish out to the bin. He made a career out of people-pleasing – the comments I heard most about Brody were: 'Isn't he helpful?' 'What a lovely boy,' and 'Thank you, Brody, you are so kind.'

I would smile weakly because I knew that Brody was a boy whose map was full of dead ends and missed turnings.

With pretty much all foster children you need to work out where the voids in their childhood map are so that you can go back and fill them in, and my own children played a really big part in this as well.

I had fostered around a hundred children by the time Brody stepped through our front door and was confident I could deal with most situations. I looked at Brody and Alfie and was convinced that I was right. They were happily playing football in the garden as though they had known each other all their lives. I smiled to myself, quietly confident that things seemed to be going in the right direction.

Chapter Three

Everything was going so well – it was the end of term, our holiday to Spain was booked and everyone was excitedly packing their suitcases. The girls' beds were strewn with bikinis of all colours, while shorts, flip-flops and sun hats littered the floor.

Holidays were a new experience for Brody, and Alfie was helping him get ready. I caught some of their conversation and heard Alfie earnestly explaining to Brody what happened when you got to the airport.

'You have to give your passport to a man to check that it's you, and then you go to a place called Duty Free where you can buy lots of stuff cheap,' Alfie said, adding, 'Do you like planes?'

'Never been on one but I'm not scared,' said Brody, who had just celebrated his seventh birthday.

When we got to Gatwick, I looked at Brody and could see that being in an airport, with all its hustle and bustle and Tannoy announcements, was freaking him out a bit. He could explode at moments like these and I hoped the bag of colouring books, word-search puzzles and sweets I'd brought with me would be enough to distract him.

I tried to think back to the first time I went on a plane so I could relate to what he was feeling. I remembered the excitement and fear as you take off, and that feeling when your stomach drops ten inches as you climb steadily into the air.

'It's a bit like being on a roller-coaster ride,' I said to Brody.

He went quiet.

'Have you ever been on a roller-coaster,' I asked.

He shook his head.

'It gives you an excited feeling in your tummy. Scary but fantastic at the same time.'

Brody nodded, but I was not at all sure he could imagine what I meant.

Once we had boarded and found our seats, I looked over at Martin, who winked at Brody as he tried to work out his seatbelt and lent over to help him.

I smiled and said, 'Honestly, it is fun.'

He nodded, but still didn't look that sure, and he closed his eyes as the plane's engines began to roar and we taxied down the runway. He didn't open them again until the plane had lifted off the ground and we had levelled out. Only then did he look apprehensively out of the window.

When the meal arrived in its little tray I could see Brody's nerves ebbing away and that he was starting to enjoy it. The flight went without a hitch, and when we landed the excitement was wonderful. I love that look on children's faces when they can't express how happy they are. Brody's face was just like that when he walked out of the cabin door. As the hot air hit him like a hairdryer, it was delightful to watch. I wished I could capture that feeling of excitement and keep it in a glass jar. I get butterflies even now just thinking about it.

The beach was right next to our apartment, so the first thing we all did was rush to our rooms, change into our swimming things, grab our towels and run down to the shore. I was sweaty from the journey and could not wait to dip my whole body into the tranquil, turquoise sea.

Brody excelled at all sports, so I assumed he would be an excellent swimmer. He ran straight into the sea, copying the other kids, so he gave me no reason to think otherwise. I was not prepared for what was about to happen, though. Suddenly, slicing through the laughter came the most piercing scream. I stopped – along with every other adult near me – to see where it was coming from, because whoever was screaming must be seriously hurt. There was no other explanation.

I saw Alfie's face and he looked horrified as he stared at Brody. It was Brody who was screaming and

I tried to run through the water towards him, the sea pushing me back with each step. By the time I reached him Martin had lifted him out and was running up the beach with him. I followed, wondering what the hell had happened. Everyone had been happy and laughing one minute and then screaming and shouting the next.

'Did something bite you?' I said as I looked at the concerned circle of adults surrounding us. Brody was still screaming out of control and couldn't talk.

'What is it?' I asked.

After a few minutes Brody managed to splutter, 'My body's on fire.' His eyes were wide and scared.

'What do you mean?' I said.

'Just help me, help me,' was all he could say.

Martin and I exchanged confused looks and Alfie sat on the sand crying, not knowing what to do. The other children looked like they had seen a ghost.

Suddenly, I remembered India, our former foster child who had no experience of the beach either and had been frightened by the feel of the sea. I realised that the salt on his skin was a sensation that was totally alien to him.

'Quick, Martin, put him under the shower.'

People were still staring, and if we'd been in Italy I could have explained in Italian what was happening, but I knew barely any Spanish and there was no way I could explain this, so I just said, 'It's okay, it's okay.'

I started to wash the salt off him, and the burning sensation gradually subsided. He slowly calmed down and eventually I wrapped him in a towel and took him back to the apartment while Martin tried to explain to Alfie what we thought had happened.

It had all become too much for the fiery little boy with his tough-guy exterior. All his bravado had melted away like chocolate in the hot sun and all that was left was a frightened lad looking at me for reassurance.

The problem foster carers face sometimes is that in the day-to-day drama of looking after these damaged children we're so wrapped up in the big stuff we forget to ask the simple questions. In this case, it was: 'Can you swim?' I hadn't even asked if he had been to the seaside before. Now that I thought about it, Brody would have already told me he was the best at swimming, because he always said he was the best at everything, even if he hadn't tried it. Back at home I had been so focused on trying to sort out Brody's school life there hadn't been much time for anything else.

I told Brody that what he thought was burning was in fact salt drying on his skin. Once he'd finally relaxed I bought him an ice cream, but it took days to get him back into the sea.

About a year after he came to live with us Brody began absconding from school on a weekly basis, so to keep him in the classroom a mentor shadowed him. But Brody was a clever opportunist, and whenever a chance arose to hop over the wall, out of the window or even over the roof, he went.

School went from bad to worse. No matter how hard we all tried to work in partnership with ideas or incentives, nothing worked. It was frustrating because Brody was very bright, but he had poor concentration and low self-esteem, which he masked with aggression and chaos. A classroom was like a prison to him – he could not apply himself to any academic session for longer than three minutes and was unable to sit still for longer than ten minutes. After that, he would disrupt the class and be sent out – a cycle that would carry on for the whole of his school life.

He had come from a chaotic household where domestic violence was a daily occurrence and the police were called regularly. The minute Brody could walk, that's what he did – he left the house to escape.

Brody adored sport, though – he was a sportsman through and through. He loved being outdoors, and I always thought he would have learned best in a farm setting. He needed somewhere to channel his energies. Having said that, we did go and stay on a farm one year but only stayed one night because Brody killed a chicken.

By the end of Brody's first year with us and the beginning of his second, home was just about manageable, although Brody was demanding and took up a lot of my time. Being in our settled household was alien to him. He had never experienced coming home from school to find a hot meal on the table, then sitting down with his family and sharing news of each other's day. Brody only knew hostility, and his independence had developed quickly. It was a fight for survival in his household – who was going to find a pound coin to get a portion of chips? Who was going to go through Dad's pockets while he lay unconscious in a drunken stupor and risk waking him up and being beaten with his belt? His mother was either dead drunk or, when she was sober, ineffectual because she was too terrified to make a decision independently – she had to get approval on every little move she made from Brody's dad.

As siblings they worked together to survive, although the older ones bullied the younger ones and a pecking order was in place from birth. Bullying was a way of life for Brody's family, a skill that was handed down from father to son.

To the outside world Brody was a small, angelic-looking child with olive skin and dark brown eyes. He was the picture of innocence, but his exterior gave no clue as to the real Brody, who was a Jekyll-and-Hyde character, dangerous and unpredictable.

Once Brody started truanting, the honeymoon was definitely over and I then realised why Lottie had greeted my enthusiasm about him with caution.

The main message Brody wanted to get across to me was that I was not, and never would be, his mother. If I showed any affection towards him at all he would freeze – rather like India had all those years ago – and when I tucked him into bed and kissed him goodnight on his forehead, he would tell me he hated me and my family.

This didn't mean much to me because for a very long time I saw Brody as a frightened little boy who was adjusting to my ever-changing family home. But in the back of my mind the ten-foot rebel with horns I'd first imagined was still lurking. To calm my fears, I often put my head round his door when he was sleeping to remind myself that he was just a little boy.

I decided to give him plenty of slack because I know how difficult it is for foster children who have been moved continually to establish trust in anyone, but he caused me no end of anguish and there were many nights when I cried myself to sleep with frustration at how I didn't seem to be getting anywhere with him. The sad thing is, I'm sure he did the same; I'm sure he cried himself to sleep wanting to be at home with his family, or because he was unable to work out why he pushed away anyone who wanted to help him. He was stuck in a loop, a hamster on a wheel, and he was getting nowhere.

I was working tirelessly to get inside Brody's world, as his behaviour was becoming increasingly unsafe, unpredictable and irrational and I was desperate to find a way to understand what was going on with him. I needed to be able to put the pieces of the jigsaw puzzle together before it was too late.

After Brody had run out of school for the umpteenth time, the film *Forrest Gump* became my inspiration. In the film, Forrest, who is a simple soul with a low IQ and a passive view of the world, starts a marathon three-year jog, running from horrible feelings he doesn't know how to deal with. He keeps on running until he sorts his head out and the feelings disappear.

I got a roll of lining paper and unrolled about twelve feet of it, stuck it on the wall and drew a long road on it.

'This is Forrest Gump's road,' I told Brody, who had watched and enjoyed the film with me.

At one end I drew his school and at the other his home in the local council estate. I stood back and looked at my wobbly road and rickety school. I was no Picasso, but at least it was clear what they were supposed to be.

'Brody.' He looked sullen and nodded at me. 'On the road from your school to your home, you must experience a lot of feelings. I'm going to cook dinner now, and when you are ready you can try to draw or write about those feelings on this map.'

As I walked away, I could hear Brody draw in a big breath, and then he started muttering. After a year of looking after him I had learned many things, and number one on the list was not to react, so I continued walking and didn't look back.

After dinner, when Brody was calm and his work was finished, I took him back to the wall and his road map, which was now covered with his squiggly writing. By the school he had written: 'I am happy when I run out of school, because I HATE doing anything anyone asks me to do.' Then he'd drawn a smiley face. 'I am happy running,' he'd written. 'I am happy to feel scared. I am happy no one can find me. I am happy when I get wobbly feelings in my stomach.'

I felt my gut knot up and was quite knocked back by these revelations. It was pretty significant that Brody had identified being scared as a happy feeling for him; shockingly, this was because it was such a familiar feeling.

Brody had spent the first three years of his life being scared and running from the violence that was normal in his house. He had to get away from that enclosed environment, and being outside away from it all was safer than being inside amongst it. The wobbly feeling in his stomach was the excitement and the adrenalin. It was a rush he loved and he was as used to this feeling of terror as another child would be to feeling happy at their own birthday party. But the saddest thing of all was that feeling safe was alien to him and made him uncomfortable.

Brody's version of Forrest Gump's road had given me a gloomy insight into the way his mind was working, and I am not afraid to admit what I saw scrawled on that wall frightened me.

I discussed Brody's road with Martin and we decided we didn't want to give up on him. But Brody gave us a bumpy ride, more hellish than any roller-coaster, and each time something went wrong I made excuses for him. 'Oh, he's having a difficult time at school. Well, he hasn't seen his parents for a few weeks.' But pretty soon I was running out of excuses, and friends started to notice that my loyalty to my family and my desire to love a lost child was becoming a battle.

The whole family were pretty dedicated when it came to helping Brody. Francesca was very close to him and often went cycling with him to try and help him understand that we all cared. Francesca was not the most tolerant of my children, so I was pleased to see this gentler side of her fiery nature. I had not witnessed her nurturing anyone so intensively before, not even her younger brother.

Later, it occurred to me that even my children had been pulled into Brody's web. He wanted 100 per cent attention 100 per cent of the time, and he had worked out how to get it.

One thing I didn't realise then was that by the time we reached the end of Brody's rocky road my heart would be broken in two.

Chapter Four

Brody's hatred towards me was developing from words to violence – he seemed to want to hurt me both physically and emotionally. The punches and kicks and the stones he threw all hurt, but nothing hurt as much as his hate.

'I HATE HER!' He would say it to anyone who would listen and I would feel the blood in my veins go cold. 'I don't want to live with you! I hate all of you!' He would spit at us at dinner sometimes.

A deathly silence would fall until someone awkwardly broke it with some inane comment. 'Help me dress my Barbies,' Ruby would pipe up, and everyone would scramble to leave the table.

What had I done that was so bad? I had loved and cared for him, sat with him when he was in such a heightened state of anger and anxiety that he was smashing anything and everything he could get his hands on. I held him when his anger vanished and cuddled him to reassure him that everything would be okay. Some nights I sat with him constantly while he had vivid nightmares and held him tight, reassuring him he was safe. He accepted my cuddles then, but let me know he still hated me the minute he felt better. I collected him from school when the teachers could no longer tolerate him. I stuck by him unconditionally, no matter what, but nothing was ever good enough. I could not give Brody what he wanted, because he did not know what he wanted himself. Feeling safe was strange to him, and while most of us would breathe easy if someone made it clear they would stick by us no matter what, it made him feel uneasy. He already knew that he was at his happiest when he was afraid, and that must have been as scary to him as it was to me.

So I became Brody's enemy, fighting a battle where there could be no winners. He had decided he was never going to let me in, and I could not work out the code to his defence system.

I refused to let it show but the hurt I felt inside was so crushing that at times I couldn't breathe. It was like invisible hands tightening round my lungs, squeezing out every last molecule of air.

I felt exhausted … physically and mentally exhausted. I became teary and withdrawn, and when I look back now I realise that, although I was an adult, I was frightened of Brody, because I was being bullied. I feel embarrassed recognising that fact, because I am a strong character and would not let a seven-foot, twenty-stone man bully me, and yet here I was being bullied by a child.

I remember feeling judged at times – never by the school, because they themselves experienced the daily abuse, but others would say to me, 'What a sweet little boy. Isn't he well mannered?' They would look at me with disbelief if ever I pointed out that he could be quite a handful.

My job as a foster carer was to try and prepare this boy for a normal life in a normal family home, with the hope of breaking the destructive cycle – a legacy from the family he had come from. But Brody went out of his way to do the opposite of everything I asked him to do, and I grew tired of the constant battles. Eventually I realised that it was easier not to ask him to do anything. After a while, he cottoned on and began to realise that I wasn't going to play his games and because of that I was, in fact, winning. This infuriated him and he began smashing up the house.

I heard the horrific sounds of crashing and banging early one evening and rushed upstairs, thinking someone had had a terrible accident. The noise was coming from Brody's room and as I opened the door I could see him in a rage, destroying everything he could get his hands on.

'Stay in your rooms, kids!' I shouted to the other children. And I stood there, in shock, powerless to do anything as he whipped through his room like a tornado.

His bunk bed went first. He battered it with a chair until it was nothing more than matchwood on the floor. Then his wardrobe got the same treatment, then his ceiling light. I was just thankful he didn't throw the chair through the window. When he'd finally finished he collapsed in an exhausted heap on the floor.

I sat next to him and silently helped him clear up the mess.

This destructive act did not go unpunished. Anything he broke I didn't replace, so his bed became a mattress on the floor, and his ceiling light was a bare bulb. Anything he broke belonging to someone else, I stopped his pocket money until he had paid for it.

Controlling Brody became impossible, though; it didn't matter what tactics I used. I was an experienced foster carer and I was close to throwing in the towel. I was constantly reminding myself that he was the child and I was the adult, but even peeping in to see him sleeping was beginning to lose its power.

Brody was definitely a product of his background and there was a part of him that was just like his father. His mum had been emotionally and physically abused by his dad, and Brody was beginning to imitate his father's behaviour towards me. He would be very rude to me in public and at home. Physical and verbal abuse came in waves and I learned to deal with it.

He told me I was a fucking bitch and to fuck off if I asked him to clean his bedroom. He would throw things at me if I asked him to do his homework, and at bedtime he would often throw punches. I began to look like a battered wife and my friends began to worry.

I became Brody's punch bag. I had been kicked and sworn at before and, looking back, it had almost become acceptable to me. I can only assume this is one reason why many women stay in abusive relationships, because the violence just doesn't seem unusual any more. I knew Brody was copying his dad's behaviour, but it did not make it acceptable.

Brody idolised his father – in the way people do idolise those they're scared of because they don't want to be on the wrong side of them – and talked about him as though he was his hero. His mother, on the other hand, was insignificant to him. He had no time for her and showed no affection towards her at all.

It was no surprise that he had a fantastic relationship with Martin and responded to him in a completely different way to how he did to me. Brody admired his father, whom he believed was a powerful man, and he respected Martin in his role as father and head of the household. He wanted to be the perfect son to Martin and in the process was becoming a cuckoo in the nest. 'Take me to football, Martin; take me to cricket, Martin; take me to tennis,

Martin.' It was subtle but brutal, and inch by inch Alfie was being pushed out.

Because Brody was so loud, so great at sports, so energetic and so eager to please Martin, and because positive behaviour was obviously something we wanted to encourage, we didn't notice that our Alfie had become second best at everything. Alfie became subdued and uncomfortable in Brody's presence. They had been best friends, as close as brothers, so I didn't consider anything was wrong with their relationship. Brothers go through good patches and bad patches, love and hate, so I thought this was the most likely scenario. That's what always happened with Francesca and Ruby anyway. They fell out all the time but always made it up in the end. I was making excuses again, but I genuinely didn't see the whole thing turning sour.

The saying that the squeakiest wheel gets oiled first is so true, and Brody knew how to dominate a room full of people. He had watched his dad do exactly the same.

I am perfectly aware of sibling rivalry – I have my own siblings either side of me – but this was different somehow. It was calculated and manipulative. Brody aimed to please, I have no doubt, but being from a large sibling group himself he had learned the art of control and domination and, without me spotting it, he was beginning to dominate Alfie. Before long, I began to notice that when Brody was in full swing people-pleasing, he would often do it when Alfie was near. 'You are such a great help,' someone would say to Brody, and he would grin and catch Alfie's eye.

Because I had seen so much potential in Brody I really wanted to help him change, because underneath it all I knew there was a really decent boy waiting to emerge and I was determined to do whatever I could to help him break out of his cocoon. All my training as a foster carer was geared towards trying to fix things for these children who had had such unlucky starts in life, and although I realised that Brody was a challenge I wanted to rise to it.

The truth was – as unlikely as it seemed to all the adults responsible for his wellbeing and care – Brody wanted to go home. He could not understand why he was not living with his mum and dad, and everything he did was geared towards getting home.

Foster children often idealise their parents and begin to blame everyone around them for their failings. I thought it was time we began talking about them honestly. His memories of home were happy ones, and I had to remind him that they were not true.

'What about that time your dad beat you with a belt and the school found out because you couldn't sit down?'

'It wasn't that bad.'

'What about all the times your dad beat up your mum and the police were called?'

'She deserved it because she was too drunk to make our tea.'

I reminded him of the number of police reports, the complaints from school and neighbours, but it had no effect. To Brody, this was normality. We were the abnormal ones.

Brody did open up on occasions. He once said, 'Mia, it's wrong to hit people, isn't it? Martin doesn't hit you, does he? Men shouldn't hit, should they?' He would have light-bulb moments where he realised his family life wasn't right. But before you knew it, he was back to playing the big man. For some children accepting your parents are incapable of acting like decent parents is too difficult. He had learned early on never to show any weakness, never to cry, and opening up to me made him feel too vulnerable. He needed to hang onto those rules and if he didn't he was being disloyal to his family. That loyalty was like a tattoo – it would take something as powerful as a laser to remove it.

My house became more and more uncomfortable as Brody realised that happy family life was a million miles from what he was used to. We were like some kind of exotic tribe to him and it was great to visit, but he wanted to be back with his own people.

The more he realised that there was never going to be a happy ending for his family, the more he rebelled. Running away gave him an adrenalin rush and that feeling of being scared that he was so used to. It was as familiar to him as being snuggled up next to Martin in a cosy, safe, warm bed was to me. And if Brody liked feeling scared I wondered how I would ever manage to cure him of his addiction.

Either I or the school were calling the police on a weekly basis, and at one point nine police cars and two helicopters were out looking for him. He had become what social workers call a 'fostering absconder', as he would run the minute he couldn't get what he wanted. 'No' was a trigger word and I tried to avoid it as best as I could. The psychologists call it 'fight or flight' and in Brody's case it was flight. The more comfortable and safe home was, the worse he became.

On the day the helicopters and police cars were out, he had run away from a happy family party. These occasions would make Brody feel particularly uncomfortable and you could see him begin to get agitated. When that happened I would try to distract him somehow until he calmed down, but on this occasion I didn't manage to get to him in time and he was out of the door faster than you could say party poppers.

By this stage he was ten, with the cunning of an eighteen-year-old. Even with all that manpower it was eight hours before the police found him. Eventually, he was spotted not far from the house hiding behind a neighbour's wall. Two officers brought him home and knocked on the door. Brody stood behind them looking defiant, refusing to say where he had been or to answer any questions.

It was a few days later when I asked him: 'Where did you go?'

'On the bus,' he said.

Brody had got on a bus, got off it, got on another bus, got off, and so on, until he'd had enough of buses. He had no idea where he had been, but he'd been riding round for hours. It was what he and his sisters did when they left their house because they could stand it no longer.

'How did you know how to get home?' I said.

'Just asked,' he replied matter-of-factly.

Brody was a fast runner, and on occasions when he absconded he would usually run and hide at the first sign of a police car. He was often found on local council estates or hiding in fields. Roaming the streets held no fear for him – why should it? He had been walking the streets all his life, so it was perfectly normal. Brody was finding that old habits were hard to break and new ones impossible to form.

It was becoming a game for Brody and a nightmare for us and all the agencies involved with him.

The family became divided. Alfie spent more and more time with his twin Isabella. Francesca and Ruby were always together anyway and Martin would care for those four, while I had my hands full with Brody and my youngest child Lucia.

Despite his aggression towards me, Brody also had an unhealthy attachment and wanted to control me. He began operating a divide and rule policy. He absolutely adored Martin, Lucia and Francesca, which compounded Alfie's misery. He wasn't that fond of Ruby, which caused problems between Ruby and Francesca, and he loved to hate me. But the fact that he had become attached to some of the family filled me with a sense of relief. At least Brody was capable of forming a close relationship with someone. I was making excuses for him again.

The truth was that our family was breaking down, but I couldn't see it. People tried to get me to see sense, but I would not listen.

'Mia, can't you see that Brody is breaking your family apart?' my mum said one day.

'It will sort itself out, Mum.'

'How do you know? Are you going to wait until you have no furniture left, Martin's left you and someone gets seriously hurt?'

'None of that is going to happen. Trust me, things will work out,' I said. But I only half believed myself.

One by one, the family gave up on Brody. No one said that I should get rid of him, and although Martin, Francesca and Lucia had a much more positive relationship with him than Alfie and Ruby, even they tried to persuade me that it wasn't working.

Ruby and Alfie had given Brody so many chances they had no more to give him. Ruby was dedicated to protecting her little brother no matter what, and being very clever she had worked Brody out long before I did. In the end, they found a solution: they stayed away from him and he stayed away from them.

Despite being treated like an infectious disease by Brody, Alfie only flipped once after Brody had gone into his bedroom and taken some of his games. When Alfie asked for them back Brody became aggressive.

'Make me,' he said, and Alfie took him on.

They started fighting and Martin managed to break it up. Alfie hated fights – we all hated fights – and when I looked at him he was shaking from head to toe. I had an overwhelming urge to cry, but I was determined I was not going to do it in front of Brody.

Still I did not want to give up on this boy whose horns were really showing now. For all Brody's faults I loved him and I knew he loved me, and I lived in hope that one day we would turn a corner and everything would be all right. But before any safe place could be reached, we were just another family at war.

It wasn't just us as a family who were struggling; the school were finding it increasingly difficult to keep Brody safe. Meetings with his form tutor and head of year had become a weekly entry in my diary and we were all running out of ideas.

'Mrs Marconi,' the head began, 'I am concerned that there is not much more we can do for Brody. We might have to consider a more secure unit.'

'But we've done so much for him, wouldn't it be a shame if we gave up now? I really do think he will turn a corner.'

'We don't share your confidence, I'm afraid.'

While I was dealing with all the dramas I couldn't see the wood for the trees. My family were the wood and I just took it for granted that they were happy to take second place for a while. Particularly Alfie – he was such a good little boy who demanded very little attention and he took a back seat without complaining so that Brody could get what he needed.

I hadn't noticed it – of course I hadn't. I was far too busy trying to sort out all the chaos and devastation that Brody seemed to leave behind him. What I wanted Brody to realise was that we weren't going to give up on him, no matter how hard he pushed us, and I thought once he realised that, everything would slot into place and he would settle into family life.

Chapter Five

Unsurprisingly, Brody's secondary-school transition did not go well. Aged just twelve, he began self-harming with pens and pencils that he would dig into his arms or legs. Then one day I took a phone call from the head teacher.

'Brody has taken a knife from the canteen. He was seen in the toilets hiding it up his sleeve.'

'I'll come and get him,' I said.

He had become aggressive and had threatened to kill himself. It was clearly a cry for help. After all, he could easily have stolen a knife from a shop during one of his unsanctioned excursions and slit his wrists somewhere secluded without anyone knowing, if that was really what he wanted to do. Brody was not a prisoner and he was not in a secure unit, and no one could monitor him twenty-four hours a day. It was easy for him to steal knives from school or from friends' houses, and the best thing we could do was to reinforce the message that he didn't need one. But it didn't matter how many times I explained that he mustn't take knives, his obsession with them continued.

I knew none of us was in danger, because it was clear that Brody was only concerned with harming himself, but still, his behaviour was extremely worrying. There was many a morning when I would find a knife under his pillow as I was making his bed. 'It's in case we get broken into and I get attacked during the night.'

It was only a matter of time before it all went wrong, and after he took a knife to school he was suspended. I reasoned that Brody was heading towards adolescence – more excuses – which I knew was a difficult time for any teenager, never mind if you had all the problems to deal with that Brody had, so I drove to the school to collect him. When we got home, I spoke to him about the dangers surrounding the whole incident. The school did its bit and identified someone for him to talk to when he wasn't coping, but he didn't bond with her and began threatening to kill himself more often.

I would sit for hours with Brody trying to get him to talk about suicide, but his usual response was to clam up. I learned it was a no-go area and played it down, waiting for him to discuss it with me. On a couple of occasions all he would say was that thinking about suicide and harming himself made him feel better. It was his private time and a time when he was in control. To us, it was a signpost that Brody was not settling and that we weren't able to provide what he needed.

A year after Brody started at secondary school Alfie followed him, and instead of having an older brother figure to look up to Alfie found being associated with Brody embarrassing. Brody was always in exclusion and Alfie did not want to be linked to a boy who was such a problem to everyone. So, soon after his first term began, Alfie started suffering a lot of little illnesses.

'Mum, I feel sick,' or 'Mum, my ear hurts,' he began saying once or twice a week, and I let him stay at home as it was so out of character for Alfie to want time off school. It was something he never asked for, so I didn't question whether he was genuinely ill or not.

It was bonding time for us when Alfie was off and we sat and talked about school, his friendships and family, and he would say if he had any problems, but Brody's name never came up.

It wasn't long before the school called to say that Alfie seemed to be taking a lot of days off sick. When I looked at his attendance record I realised he'd had a lot of time at home, so I asked for a meeting with the school. I thought something must have been happening there; maybe there was a teacher he didn't get on with or he wasn't enjoying being at senior school. I knew that it could take time to settle down in year seven and was sure it was just teething trouble.

The school said they had no concerns and were unable to flag anything up other than that Alfie seemed quiet sometimes. Things were beginning to seem odd at home too, because Alfie had also become quieter and quieter there. When his behaviour wasn't withdrawn, he was beginning to have angry outbursts.

'I get butterflies when Brody is around, Mum.'

'Why?' I asked. 'I don't know,' he said.

'Have a good think about it and see if you can work it out.'

'I will,' he said, but he never talked of it again.

What we had no idea of was what was happening behind all our backs. Brody was taking his anger out on Alfie, and to cope Alfie was taking his anger out on us. In my ignorance I put it down to his age, and so did the family.

'He doesn't want to grow up,' my mum suggested.

'It's just his age,' said my brother.

And at times I did wonder whether Alfie was trying to copy Brody.

Martin began spending more time with Alfie, playing football and tennis with him. It was partly because Brody was getting to that age where he had his own friends and was going out with them after school, meeting them at local clubs or in the wood nearby.

Then one night I had a really odd conversation with Alfie when I was tucking him into bed.

'Night, Alfie,' I said.

'Can you ask my teacher if I can be on report?' he said out of the blue.

'Why would you want to be on report? It's not good to be on report,' I said.

'Yes it is, because when Brody comes off report at school they give him a present.'

I was totally taken aback. 'I know, Alfie, but believe me being on report is not a good thing, it truly isn't. They are just trying to reward Brody for good behaviour.'

He grunted and rolled his eyes.

I kissed him and said, 'Mummy loves you,' but he didn't reply.

The following Monday Alfie was off school again with a stomach ache while Lottie was visiting. Brody was having therapy sessions at home with me by this stage. Once a week, at lunchtime, a family psychologist would come in and sit with us to try and help us turn our relationship around, or at least get to the bottom of what was making Brody so aggressive towards me. He hated those sessions, and they seemed only to be making things worse.

After the session Brody would not go back to school. Lottie would sometimes visit to talk to us both about how it had all gone, but today she came in, sat down and looked at Alfie. She threw me a knowing look and then went over to the sofa to sit with him.

I went to make a cup of tea while Lottie put her arm around Alfie's shoulders.

'What's going on at school?' she asked gently.

Before Alfie had a chance to answer, Brody demanded that Lottie watch him perform a backflip on the trampoline and the moment was lost.

It was a Thursday, a day like any other. The kids were home from school; they'd had their tea and were settling down to do their homework at the kitchen table. All except Brody.

'Brody, you need to do your homework,' I said, using the singsong voice I usually used when I wanted to make things sound like fun.

'Fuck off!' he said, and bolted for the door.

Brody was so quick he had disappeared before I could cross the kitchen to reach him.

I knew the routine – I would have to get the car out and go hunting the streets. I asked Alfie to come with me and we drove around places where we thought he would be: the woods, his family's council estate, and then I turned into a local field where the kids used to kick a football around. A rock hit the windscreen. I ducked and pulled Alfie's head down. As I lifted my head again I saw Brody running away, so I got out of the car.

'Brody! Get in the car!' I shouted. He stopped and just stared and laughed at me, turned round and started running again. I got back in the car, shaking, and looked over at Alfie, who was crying.

'I'm scared, Mum,' he said.

Suddenly, it hit me like a bolt of lightning – Brody was bullying Alfie. How could I have been so stupid and not seen it? I only had to look at the panic-stricken look on Alfie's face and the situation became clear. I hugged him.

'Don't worry. You're safe. I won't let Brody hurt you any more.'

Those words 'any more' made all the difference. Without me having to say it directly, Alfie knew that I had worked out what I should have worked out months before. He breathed a sigh of relief.

All I wanted to do was to get my son out of there, so I picked up my phone, called the police and explained the situation. They took my location and said calmly, 'Someone is on the way.'

'I need to leave, so I won't be here.'

'It's fine, ma'am. We'll take care of it.'

An hour later the police arrived at my house, having picked up Brody along with Lottie from social services. I was so livid I didn't want Brody in the house, so he sat in the car. I looked at him and you could tell he was still in a rage. He gave me a look of pure hatred, but by that stage I was past caring and I gave him a look back.

I had asked Lottie to come.

'I need a break, Lottie,' I said. I wanted time to reflect on what had happened and needed to support Alfie. I was now in an impossible situation where I was trying to save someone else's child, and in the process it seemed like I was damaging my own. This was different to our foster child Hope dying – death is an inevitable part of life, even when it's premature. It is devastating if it happens, but you can move on. This was different, this was abuse. This was not what fostering was about, I told myself. I knew that my children put their hearts and souls into improving family life for youngsters who had been badly treated by the very people who should love and care for them the most, but what I had seen had convinced me that my son was suffering physical and emotional abuse in return.

Lottie nodded and did not argue. 'I will start the paperwork to get you some respite,' she said.

My heart ached for my son and hardened towards Brody. I was dreading what would happen next, but I knew I needed a break from Brody and I'm sure he felt the same.

When the police finally brought him inside, I did not want to look him in the eyes. For six years we had tried with him, but his road map had shown quite clearly that he wanted to be at home with his parents and siblings, however terrible his life was there, and it seemed that nothing was going to persuade him otherwise.

Chapter Six

I got my respite and Brody went to stay with another foster family for a week. While he was away I thought about how to deal with his relationship with Alfie. It would do neither of them any good if we just walked away, so our family and social services would have to find a way to help them work it out. Alfie would meet other bullies in life, and Brody needed to learn that bullying was wrong and could seriously harm others.

When Brody returned, he seemed different. 'Maybe he's missed us?' I thought, but I think he knew that he had almost pushed us too far. I was tempted to let my guard down a little, but I didn't. Time would tell if Brody was really planning on turning a corner, or whether he was planning another assault, but for now we would take it day by day and try to carry on as normal.

Social services are like any boss – they make good and bad decisions. The first bad decision they made, in my opinion, was leaving Brody with his parents for so long, but the one that would affect him – and us – irreparably was his trip to army camp in Dorset. Brody was nearly thirteen and he had joined the Territorial Army cadets. It was his first trip and he would be away for a weekend. Martin took him shopping to the local camping store and bought him all the equipment he would need, including walking boots, a rucksack and a sleeping bag. Then the following Friday he dropped him off at the local army barracks. It was to be a three-day excursion and afterwards we all planned to fly off to Italy for the summer.

Brody was really excited, and so was I. I thought this would be a really positive experience for him.

I helped him pack and as he left I gave him £50, just like I would have done to any of my own children, but that night I received a phone call from the camp asking me to come and pick Brody up. He had smashed all the other kids' lockers open and stolen their money. 'Even the Army can't contain him,' I thought. They wanted him to come home but this time I knew I'd had enough.

'I can't pick him up,' I said stiffly to the sergeant, 'and my partner is working. Social services will have to deal with it.'

When Lottie arrived at the barracks, the police were there and she spent two hours filling out paperwork. When she finally brought Brody home I asked for a meeting and said that, as a family, we were not happy taking Brody to Italy as he was becoming more and more unpredictable.

Lottie saw my point but her boss didn't. She told Lottie to tell me that I was expected to take him with us. I was adamant and knew I had reached breaking point. 'I can't risk my family's safety any longer,' I said – I can be stubborn when I want to be. 'We are not taking him with us.'

I couldn't believe the words had come out of my mouth, but now they had a sense of relief crept into my bones. We were going on holiday without Brody and that was that. I allowed myself a small smile.

Social services took me at my word and the next day Brody was sent to stay with my lovely friend Kathy. Kathy is a short-term foster carer and Brody would stay with her until we came home.

I broke the news to Brody, who went berserk and told me he didn't want to live with us any more anyway. I'm sure it was all bluff and bluster, but if a child says something like that I have to report it.

I called Lottie and told her what Brody had said. She spoke to her boss, Trudi, whom I expected to say that social services would talk to Brody and explain to him the seriousness of what he had done, but instead of backing me up and telling him that he had to take responsibility for his actions, she said, 'Well, if that's what he wants …'

I thought this was a recipe for disaster: now Brody knew he could do exactly what he wanted and not face any consequences. He could cause havoc and just walk away and leave a horrific mess behind. But the decision had been made. It was out of my hands. Brody would leave us permanently and he would leave immediately.

It was quite late by now, so the girls put the younger children to bed. I packed up Brody's belongings – not in black bin liners like when he'd arrived, but in his rucksack and another case we had bought him for when we went on holiday. By the time I handed Brody's bags to Lottie, the kids were all asleep.

Lottie was ready to take him away. 'Bye, Brody,' I said. Brody looked at me with undisguised hatred and I shivered. He turned and left without saying a word and I thought that would be the last time I ever saw him.

That night he moved to Kathy's, where he stayed until the morning before absconding. After he was found, he was then moved out of the area so that he was nowhere near our house.

Placements mostly break down when foster carers are absolutely exhausted and no one is listening to or supporting them when they need it most. I felt as though I was in that position now. This is not always the fault of the social worker, and Lottie had been fantastic, but she could not overrule her boss Trudi, who seemed not to have grasped the situation. Or maybe she knew something I didn't. She had only seen Brody on two occasions but had taken the decision that after six years it was time for him to leave us. All I had asked for was respite care so that we could go on a family holiday; I hadn't wanted Brody to leave permanently, but the situation had escalated and Brody was now losing his home. I thought it was a bad move at the time, but honestly, with hindsight, although I couldn't swear it was the right choice for Brody, I think Trudi made the right choice for us.

Even so, I was devastated. I had looked after a hundred children by the time Brody came to live with us. Some had stayed months and years and some just days and weeks, but in all that time only one placement had broken down. At the time, I had been distraught and consumed by 'what ifs' and 'if onlys', and this time was no different.

Now Brody had gone, and the funny thing was, the day after he absconded, Trudi left social services herself.

The next morning I explained to the kids that Brody was not going to live with us any more. There was silence for a minute while they took in what I was saying. Ruby, Isabella and Alfie were delighted, while Martin, Francesca and Lucia were sad. But we'd had years of police coming in and out of our home, and the worst thing was that we had become used to it. That was no way to live, I thought, and not what we wanted.

'What, he's never coming back?' said Ruby.

'Never?'

'What, never, ever, ever?' said Alfie.

'Never, ever, ever.'

Alfie turned away and smiled to himself with relief. I knew I would need a long chat with him, but for now Italy was my priority.

My news had not had as much impact as it could have as we were all excited about the holiday and ready to leave for the airport, but I could tell by everyone's faces that, whether they were happy or sad, they were definitely relieved.

Brody had dominated my life for six years and without me realising it he had stripped me of everything. I would never have been able to give Brody enough. No matter how much I gave him, he wanted more. He was a powerful presence, one that deafened me to the alarm bells and the warnings of my friends and family.

I was physically and mentally wrecked, so much so that I actually felt ill. My body, my mind and my heart were exhausted from the constant torment that I had given up on a child. Nothing had ever felt so wrong, and the impact was taking its toll.

I thought about all the children who had been part of our family and who had left happy, with a chance of living a fulfilled, normal life, and I felt a failure. It was a feeling like no other: heavy, over-whelming, destructive. I had given up on a child and I had no idea how I would come to terms with that. It didn't matter that I kept telling myself how impossible Brody had been and how I – and my whole family – had tried everything. Good foster carers before and after me had all tried and we had all failed. So I consoled myself with the thought that Brody just wanted to be at home, however awful it was, and no one was going to derail him from his first and final destination.

As we boarded the plane I could feel a lightness around my shoulders, as if ten tons of bricks had been lifted. I felt so light I could have flown myself if I'd had wings. When you are surrounded by stress and chaos it becomes the normality of your life, and it's not until you escape its grasp that you realise what a powerful presence it was and how it drained everything from you: your courage, your spirit, your faith. My character, which had always been so strong and buoyant, had become weak and broken.

I looked at my family. We all looked frazzled and lifeless. Our batteries were flat. Most of all we needed to be far away from anything that reminded us of Brody. We needed to recharge in peace.

The plane landed, the cabin doors opened and as we began to descend the steps to the runway, that familiar heat hit us like someone had just opened the oven door. All at once, our faces came alive.

The four-week holiday that we took every year near my dad's old home was a healing experience for us all and it could not have come at a better time. I slept for almost a week and each time I tried to get out of bed my legs buckled. I just had to give in to rest.

Martin and the kids brought me cups of tea and I got up for meals, but after I had eaten I would feel the exhaustion hit me like a tidal wave and would sleep again for another eight hours.

It was on the eighth day that I finally woke up feeling refreshed. I was up and back on my feet, taking part in family life again. It was slightly alien at first as I learned to give the other children attention and to take time for me – something I had been unable to do for years.

Martin and I, always the best of friends, sat in silence, hand in hand, and watched the sea. We had missed each other and were rekindling our love and friendship. I read with the kids and swam and laughed with them. We did simple things like eat pizza on the beach at midnight, collect mussels from the rocks and pick oranges and figs from the trees, and we did it together without the pervasive presence of Brody demanding all of my attention. How had I allowed Brody to take over my life, I asked myself? Where had it gone wrong? I had no concrete answers.

We had family chats about Brody, although not for long periods of time – I didn't want that. This was our time and Brody was not going to spoil it for us.

None of us hated or judged Brody, which might sound strange, because we realised that life was hard for him. What we mostly felt was sorrow and relief. I had been waiting for a turning point with Brody, a chance to help him move on with his life and build a strong foundation, but the opportunity never came. At the beginning of the holiday I felt nothing but guilt about this, but by the end, once I'd talked it all through with Martin, I felt free. I was finding myself again.

Chapter Seven

It was about a week after we got home that I sat in Alfie's bedroom on his bed, handed him a cup of hot chocolate and began to talk to him.

'You have to tell me what has been going on. You don't need to be scared – Brody's gone and he's not coming back, but I know he's been bullying you and you need to tell me everything.'

Alfie broke down, shaking from head to toe, crying like I had never seen him cry before. I held him for what seemed like half an hour, until his sobs subsided and he was able to talk.

'When Brody first arrived, Mum, I was so excited to find out about his hobbies and he was excited to find out about me. It was great when I discovered we both liked football and I loved him straight away. It was like having my best friend around every day.

'Remember, we were at different schools at first, and I would rush home to see him and then we would go off in the garden for hours. It was like having a brother.

'Then he changed. I could never understand why he got angry with you. I hated it when he was abusive and it made me feel angry, but I knew that I was just a kid and there was nothing I could do.

'I don't know why but when Brody started at secondary school he got worse. When he came home from school he used to take all his anger and frustration out on me. He would take things from my room, then hit me when I asked for them back. Mum, it was like he was constantly trying to overpower me.'

I felt completely cold and went as white as a sheet. I began to feel sick as Alfie continued his story.

'He got so competitive, Mum. He would repeat over and over and over again, "I'm a better footballer than you. I'm a better runner than you. I'm a better cricketer than you." When you and Dad weren't around he made horrible comments. He said I was useless, ugly and an idiot. He was always trying to put me down, but he was clever and called me names when he knew no one would hear. No matter how hard I tried, he just treated me as though I was a problem.

'Most of the time I just let it go over my head, but sometimes I got so frustrated I cried myself to sleep.'

I felt a single tear start to creep down my cheek.

'I don't know what's happened to me, Mum. I feel like I don't exist any more, that nothing I do matters and that no one is interested in me. I don't know why I've let him get on top of me.'

Alfie went on to say how he could see that Brody running away was upsetting me and how he really felt for me having to spend so much time driving round the streets looking for him. He told me how when the police visited, which was on a regular basis, he used to hide upstairs.

'Why?' I asked him.

'I don't know,' he said. 'Just scared, I guess.'

I looked at the anxiety etched on my son's face and felt the heat burn my own. I held him tightly and told him that he didn't need to worry any longer, because Brody was NEVER coming back into our house.

'You never have to see him any more, Alfie.'

'What about at school?' he said.

I felt numb. I had forgotten about school. How long would it be before another school was found that could take Brody? Months, as it turned out.

So things got worse before they got better, and the effect on Alfie was awful to watch. He had more days off sick, his work was beginning to suffer and he became more and more withdrawn.

Although Brody had moved to another foster family outside the area, it was three months in the end until they found him a new school.

At school, he showed no compassion for Alfie. There was no respite from the taunts and torments – in fact, the bullying got worse. He continued to call Alfie names – 'sissy boy', 'gay boy' – and threatened to beat him up. Alfie is not a fighter. Even though it was clear he was going to be tall, and his height would have intimidated some, he hated violence and avoided it at any cost.

He faked every illness going, even a broken leg at one point, and the majority of the time I kept him at home because I knew what was happening at school. When he did go to school he would be constantly calling me on his phone, asking to come home, and I would often go and pick him up. When he made it to the end of the school day I made sure I collected him, but I didn't go to the front gate, I waited round the corner. The last thing Alfie needed was Brody calling him 'Mummy's boy' or 'pansy boy'. But the day finally came when Brody moved schools and at last Alfie was free.

Once Brody was out of Alfie's life for good, Martin and I made a concerted effort to help Alfie rebuild his confidence. We had plenty of one-on-one time with him, we had his friends for special camping sleepovers in the garden, we took him to the cinema and then for pizza afterwards, and all the time we pointed out his achievements and the strong points in his personality. Little by little I could see his confidence returning until eventually he rejoined the rough and tumble of family life.

I knew why Brody had targeted Alfie and why he had made him his whipping boy. He could not accept that his own behaviour was his own fault and he needed someone to blame. Alfie was the obvious choice. Brody was in denial, and did not know how to take responsibility for his actions. Nothing helped him or had any effect. Not the sanctions, not the love and attention, and not Alfie's friendship. All had failed. Brody had failed and he knew it, so he took it out on the one person he knew would not fight back.

Deep down Brody wanted everything Alfie had: a mum and dad who loved him unconditionally, sisters he could have a close relationship with, a clean home and an extended family that could be relied upon. Instead, his family lived in squalor, all his sisters were pregnant by the time they were fifteen, his mother had a drink problem, his father was abusive and his extended family consisted of his mother's ex-partners as far as I could work out.

After he ran away from Kathy's, Brody went to live with an elderly couple whose children were grown up and had left home. I liked them but wondered how they were going to deal with his energy. Each morning, Brody was instantly wide awake as soon as he opened his eyes and was full on until he went to sleep. His days consisted of constant demands for pats on the back and attention. Brody was like the Duracell bunny; his battery never ran down. By this time, however, I had no energy left to worry about it. It was out of my hands, and alongside the regret all I felt was relief.

It was six months later when I heard that Brody had been moved from the old couple's home. He had hit one of the grandchildren and she had fallen and broken her arm. Once he had left, the grandchildren had all said how he had been bullying them, but not one of them had said anything before. Bullying was part of Brody's survival kit – it was rooted in his psyche, planted there long before he came into care, and I wondered if he would ever control it or whether he would become just like his dad.

Chapter Eight

The following New Year's Eve, at exactly midnight, the phone rang. I was expecting it to keep ringing with various family members who were not at my house calling to scream, 'HAPPY NEW YEAR!' I picked up the phone and for a moment could not make out the voice. The family were singing 'Auld Lang Syne' in the kitchen at the tops of their voices, so I took the phone into the garden. It felt rude to say, 'Who is it?' so I stayed quiet and waited for the caller to speak.

'Are you having another party?' the caller said.

I sat on a garden chair in shock, looking at my house full of people laughing and dancing as I recognised Brody's voice.

'Is that you, Brody?'

'Yes. Who did you think it was?'

'Well, I haven't heard from you in a while. How are you?'

'I'm doing well, Mia. I just wanted to say Happy New Year to you and all the family.' I stayed silent for a minute while I took this in.

'I really am so happy you called,' I said eventually. 'It's the best start to a new year I could have.'

Brody giggled. 'I'll call you soon, Mia. Gotta go. Me mates are waiting.'

'Bye, Brody. Take care of yourself.'

'Bye, Mia.' Then the line went dead.

I sat in silence looking at the big oak tree at the bottom of my garden, taking time to realise just how beautiful it was. I took a deep breath and smiled as I felt my heart expanding with happiness. It was great to hear from him because, despite everything, all I wanted for Brody was a happy ending.

I walked back into the hum of our party and looked at all the children dancing and laughing. These were moments that I cherished, but there was something else. That one phone call meant that I had made a difference to Brody. I had taught him to forgive. The last time I'd seen him he'd given me a look of such unadulterated hate that I was in no doubt I would never hear from him again. Now, a year later, Brody was at a place on his road where he felt safe enough to call me.

Intermittently from then on I received the odd text from him. 'Hi Mia, its Brody. How r u? It wld be grt to c u.' After the first one I told social services and asked if I could see him.

'He's fine,' they said, 'but we think it will unsettle him if you have contact.'

I could have understood better if it had been me trying to contact him, but he was contacting me saying that he missed me and would like to see me. Neither of us was angry any more, so surely it was safe enough to meet?

Brody continued calling me and texting occasionally, and I would let social services know when I heard from him, but they always felt that for us to meet up would be disruptive. I could see their point and accepted their decision, although it was frustrating not to have closure. Supervised contact might have worked for both of us, just to clear the air. After all, Brody had stayed with us for six years – the longest he had stayed with any of his foster families – and he clearly had things he wanted to say, although I doubted that 'sorry' was one of them.

We spoke on the phone and I was grateful for his messages – which were strangely healing to me – and to know that he was okay. We even laughed on occasions. The conversations were never very deep. He would ask how the girls were and was pleased to hear that they were doing well, but he never once asked about Alfie. Never.

School never did work for Brody and he left with no qualifications. His only focus was getting home, and that was more important to him than trying to get an education. Family is so powerful, and until it's taken away from you, you never really appreciate the hold it has over you. I'm sure a psychologist would be able to explain it, but all I understood from some of the children who had lived with me was that, however chaotic their parents were, they still wanted to be with them. As amazing as it may seem, I had discovered that this was the rule rather than the exception. Our yearning to hang onto our roots is so strong because without them we have no foundation. We become a house of cards that can collapse at any minute. But if those foundations are rotten, our house still falls down, so what was the answer? I didn't know.

When Brody was fifteen he ran away from his seventh foster family. He kept running away until social services accepted that he was safe to be living at home with his mum and dad. They visited him regularly and monitored his progress, and he seemed happy.

We met once after his eighteenth birthday and I asked him about the stone-throwing incident. He said he could remember absolutely nothing about it, and I believed him because at the time he was in a different zone to us. Alfie, however, remembers absolutely everything about that evening.

It would be years before I accepted that, really, there was nothing I could have done differently to help Brody. The cold, hard facts were – and he'd drawn this quite clearly as a ten-year-old boy on his Forrest Gump map – that he wanted to be at home with his dysfunctional family. His loyalty to them was so strong he needed to sabotage anyone and anything that might take him away from them. Brody could not accept that life could be good for him. I suppose he was like my uncle, sent off to public school to get a good education and a good job, and, to outsiders, he seemed to get a better life. But he committed suicide because he no longer fitted the family blueprint. He was alienated from the people he loved once he was on a different level to them, and it put him in a lonely place. Brody faced the same kind of alienation if he conformed and began to fit in with society. There was no guarantee for him that he could start a brand-new life.

There were children who were so relieved to be away from their abusive families that they reinvented themselves and totally moved away, but they were the exception. Most of them wanted to have contact with their families, they just wanted them to behave better, and when they didn't change they threw in the towel and settled down to a life of drink and drugs to deal with it, and so the cycle went on.

Brody is just at the beginning of his journey – a young man with no qualifications, a chaotic family and not much hope for the future. But all that was his choice and one that, for the moment, he seems happy with. In one of the last texts he sent he said: 'You see, I got what I wanted.'

I've come to realise that life teaches us many things and that our experiences mould us into the adults we become. Little things that don't seem important at the time emerge from our memories years later, and we begin to understand that they happened for a reason.

I have struggled at times with the decisions I have made and the heartache my kids have endured because of my decision to care for damaged children, but I console myself with the knowledge that with each foster child who came into our home, we learned as much from them as they did from us, and as a family we cope with the world much better because of that.

My children have learned that the simple things they take for granted, like Christmas turkey and birthday celebrations, are in fact not a normal part of life for many children, and so they really appreciate the little things in life.

As a child I once eavesdropped on my grandmother, listening to her from behind the door. I heard her say that forgiveness is a gift that comes with age. I didn't understand what she meant then, but now I do. And I have learned to forgive Brody, as hard as it was.

As a family, we have learned to forgive and forget, to embrace differences and accept challenges without judging. This might seem like a small thing, but it's not; it's huge. My children share their love, time and kindness without hesitation, and that is a big thing to ask of anyone.

if Only He'd Told Me

At low points, when I weep into my pillow with guilt, I have to remind myself how beautiful and wonderful my children have become. They have a unique quality of not discriminating against people in any way, and one thing is certain: they have plenty of hair-raising stories to tell their own children.

Now Brody is back with his family I have faith that I and my family, and particularly Alfie, made a difference to his life, and he can hold onto that as he grows up.

We were made with two ears and one mouth for a reason and that is because listening is more important. A few years ago I asked Alfie why he hadn't told me earlier about his unhappiness. He said, 'I did, Mum, but you just weren't listening.' I instantly remembered our conversation when he told me about the butterflies in his stomach and wondered why I didn't probe deeper then. He was right. I was not ready to hear. I was the one in denial.

Despite what happened with Brody, we, as a country, take a lot of pride in fostering children and doing it well. My training is intense, and although you occasionally hear of the odd bad apple in foster care, the vast majority of carers are dedicated to making a difference. We cherish moments with the children who come into our homes. We hold their hands when they need us, tuck them into bed and reassure them that they are safe, and then do the same again after they've had a nightmare. We stand in the rain while they play football or netball, rearrange our schedules so we can attend parents' evenings and school plays, and we do what most parents do without thinking: we love and we care and we nurture.

But when your extended family no longer feels happy and normal, and the reason you are fostering becomes unclear, and your home seems an alien environment and your own children begin to suffer, it is time to question what good you are doing and ask whether you are helping at all.

As a family, we have had so many positive placements, which is why Brody leaving us was such a big deal. He just did not want to fit into our family, which left Alfie and me heartbroken. I remained angry, hurt and wounded for months, but I slowly regained my energy and enthusiasm. Alfie, on the other hand, still cannot forgive years later. They were dark, dark days for him, and although he learned from the experience he is not ready to absolve Brody.

Brody continued to move around until he eventually went home. He and I have spoken a number of times since his New Year's Eve phone call, and during one of our conversations he said something that explained exactly why he had done the things that he had done. He said simply: 'Mia, living with you were some of the best days of my life, but I just wanted to go home.'

Harper True.

Time to be inspired

Write for us

Do you have a true life story of your own?

Whether you think it will inspire us, move us, make us laugh or make us cry, we want to hear from you.

To find out more, visit

www.harpertrue.com or send your ideas to harpertrue@harpercollins.co.uk and soon you could be a published author.